Intentional LIVING

30 Productivity Principles to Achieve Peace of Mind

Intentional LIVING

30 Productivity Principles to Achieve Peace of Mind

DR. JATUN DORSEY

purposely created
PUBLISHING

INTENTIONAL LIVING

Published by Purposely Created Publishing Group™

Copyright © 2017 Dr. Jatun Dorsey

All rights reserved.

No part of this book may be reproduced, distributed or transmitted in any form by any means, graphics, electronics, or mechanical, including photocopy, recording, taping, or by any information storage or retrieval system, without permission in writing from the publisher, except in the case of reprints in the context of reviews, quotes, or references.

Printed in the United States of America

ISBN: 978-1-945558-12-2

Special discounts are available on bulk quantity purchases by book clubs, associations and special interest groups. For details email: sales@publishyourgift.com or call (888) 949-6228

For information logon to: http://www.publishyourgift.com/

Photographer: Nikki G. Productions

Make-up: Monai' Artistry

DISCLAIMER

The purpose of this book is to educate and inspire change.

The author and publisher shall have neither liability nor responsibility to any loss or damage caused, directly or indirectly, by the information contained in this book. Your success is predicated upon your work ethic, will to impose a mindset shift, and consistency implementing the principles shared in this work. We cannot and do not make result guarantees or give legal advice.

Dedication

I dedicate this book to my husband, Floyd Dorsey, for being my guiding light, life partner, and trusted sounding board. I could never thank you enough for how you challenge me and, even more so, for how you love me. You continue to play a starring role in my life and business.

Table of Contents

Acknowledgments ix

About This Book xii

Introduction..1

SHIFT YOUR MINDSET 5
Principle #1 – Create Capacity 6
Principle #2 – Don't Feel Accomplished By Mere Intentions 9
Principle #3 – Distractions Are Like Contractions.................. 11
Principle #4 – Develop Rituals.................................... 14
Principle #5 – Closed Mouths Don't Get Fed 19
Principle #6 – Do More Than Get It, Keep It.......................... 21
Principle #7 – It's Hard To See The Picture When You Are
   In The Frame.. 23

DON'T FAIL TO PLAN 25
Principle #8 – Ask The Right Questions................................. 28
Principle #9 – Don't Reinvent The Wheel 31
Principle #10 – Master One Task At A Time 35
Principle #11 – Know Your "Why"... 39
Principle #12 – There's Never A Perfect Moment 43
Principle #13 – Fail To Plan, Plan To Fail................................. 46

MAKE EVERY MINUTE COUNT ... 49
Principle #14 – Maintain A Trusted System ... 50
Principle #15 – Timing Is Everything ... 52
Principle #16 – Devote Time ... 54
Principle #17 – Low-Hanging Fruit ... 56
Principle #18 – You Touch It, You Finish It ... 58

MAKE IT HAPPEN ... 61
Principle #19 – Documentation Beats Conversation ... 62
Principle #20 – Clarity Is King ... 66
Principle #21 – Slow It Down To Break It Down ... 69
Principle #22 – Organize, Don't Agonize ... 72
Principle #23 – Schedule Your Priorities ... 75
Principle #24 – Align Your Tongues ... 78

REFILL YOUR TANK ... 81
Principle #25 – When You Grow Tired, Rest, Don't Quit ... 82
Principle #26 – Family First, No Exceptions ... 86
Principle #27 – Dedication To Meditation ... 89
Principle #28 – Know Your Limit ... 92
Principle #29 – Be Open To Change ... 96
Principle #30 – Celebrate Wins ... 100

Conclusion ... 103

About the Author ... 105

References ... 107

Acknowledgments

I am convinced that my purpose in life is to influence, encourage, and support growth and bigger thinking. I do not take this assignment lightly and, therefore, will consistently pursue projects like these to continue my work on earth.

To my husband, Floyd—God truly proved to me that I was one of his favorites by making me your wife. Your love, support, and consistency have carried me through, and for that, I appreciate you.

To my parents, Bobby and Jacquelyn: Thank you for your unconditional love. You always instilled commendable habits and expectations that ultimately positioned me for success.

To my family and friends: I appreciate your support and understanding as I continue to grind toward my endeavors.

I am ever so grateful to God for entrusting me with such a delicate duty, teaching others how to dream and act on those dreams. There is not enough wind in me to offer enough thanks to the Creator for preparing me to show up in the world unapologetically, as the best me. Thank You for empowering me with the will and tenacity to function in high performance to produce my accomplishments. Now, I am more than equipped to share the principles I live by.

About This Book

I have written this book to help make your journey toward increased productivity easier. It is important that you do not rush the process, because habits, good and bad, require time and patience to create, and even more to break. My hope is that these thirty principles will offer you the guidance necessary to get into action and remain committed to implementation. Remember that you don't have to go at this alone: The process of growth always works best when you have an accountability partner who wants to see you win. With that, I encourage you to share this information with others, collaborate, and dominate your dreams, goals, and lives together.

This book is segmented into five simple steps: "Shift Your Mindset," "Don't Fail to Plan," "Make Every Minute Count," "Make it Happen," and "Refill Your Tank." Each section has a number of principles to help you reframe your thoughts, outline a goal plan, take advantage of the time you have, make moves, and serve from your overflow. Regardless of your age, gender, or where you are in life, I am confident that you will be inspired to implement change.

While reading, reflect on the "Productive Ponders" associated with each principle and take action. Each question is designed to organize your thinking around the implementation of each topic, since, as a whole, this book is meant to ignite thought, leadership, and action in your life unlike you have ever experienced before. If you stick with the process and implement, you will realize the results you want. You are not alone: Referencing my own experiences throughout, I will offer analogies for more clarity and guidance. These are the many rituals that I commit to in order to remain on track toward my goals and in alignment with my destiny.

So if you are ready to change the way you have always done things and earn a more fulfilling life, grab a pen, a highlighter, and a notepad. Find a quiet spot and enjoy the journey toward living intentionally.

Introduction

At some point in life, many of us have found ourselves unprepared, wasting time, procrastinating, feeling underserved, and being overwhelmed. Perhaps you've felt this way for most of your life. We ignore the many signs that tell us we should do things differently and we continue functioning in a state that hinders us. As a result, we find ourselves stressed, depressed, unfulfilled, and empty. No one wins when you are not right within.

This book outlines key principles that I have used, and continue to use, in my life to remain at peace while working toward my goals. I now understand that life is made up of distractions and there is nothing constant but change—this knowledge has been a great reference tool to overcome the speed bumps in life.

As a life and business coach, I work with clients to increase productivity while maintaining peace of mind. I encourage them to get unstuck and into consistent action, and to say yes to themselves. Over the years, I have noticed that the common problem for many people is that they allow themselves to come in last place in their own lives. They are not playing the leading role. In most cases, they prioritize other people and things to maintain an image, keep the "peace," or satisfy others. Before they know it, a significant amount of time has expired and they find themselves lost in others while completely unfamiliar with self. Their dreams and aspirations have been ignored and neglected at the expense of others, and mostly by choice.

It is at this point of realization that people often discover one of the following: They have no idea what they want out of life or they know what they want but are not sure how to get into action. Either way, it is important to be clear, have accountability, and get into consistent action.

We must begin first by identifying what is stopping us from moving forward: Some struggle with taking the first step. Hesitation in stepping out is often a result of fear of the unknown. Fear will absolutely cause people to die with their dreams still in them.

Meanwhile, there are others who do not create plans and allow themselves to be controlled by the days instead of utilizing each day to implement and follow well thought-out plans. Many use the excuse that there just isn't enough time. Well, we all have the same twenty-four hours and plenty have used them to become a success in their own right. Those of us who get stuck at the stage of consistent action often do not begin with a mindset shift in the first place: You must change how you think of yourself and your goals, reframe your thoughts into "positives" and "musts."

And finally, many are unproductive because they are simply worn out from doing so much of what they do not enjoy, only to satisfy others. It is important to fill your cup and serve from your overflow—when you give, give from not the stress in you, but from the best in you.

By shifting your mindset, setting a plan, taking advantage of the time you have, making consistent action, and refilling your tank along the way, you will produce the goals that you aspire to achieve. When you are focused on these things, there are no distractions, roadblocks, or negative thoughts that can keep you from success. With that being said, all things take time and all things worth the end result require effort. Now, it is up to you to detach from whatever holds you back so that you may gracefully walk into who you are destined to be.

SHIFT YOUR MINDSET

"Change the way you look at things and the things you look at will change."

—Dr. Wayne Dyer

Principle #1 – Create Capacity

Your mindset is what causes you to do or not do, to feel confident or insecure. Everything about you is derived from how and what you think. Therefore, if you find yourself constantly engaging in negative self-talk and doubting your own abilities, then that is exactly what will manifest in your life. An African Proverb says, "If there is no enemy within, the enemy without can do you no harm." If you develop the habit of thinking with high vibrations, you create a positive energy that will become who you are. Once that energy is strong and unbreakable, there is no chance that anything or anyone can come along and break your confidence.

Changing your mindset creates capacity for you to grow, to let go of people and things that deter or distract you from your goals. Many struggle with being productive in life and business because they talk themselves out of it before anyone else has a chance to tell them they cannot achieve a thing. Naysayers come in all forms and may be someone close to you. Be prepared. In order to armor yourself, you must reframe your thoughts, which, in turn, will create the mental and physical capacity you need to succeed.

Now, reframing your thoughts requires practice. When you sense any ounce of negative self-chatter or any thought that is not indicative of your greatness, adjust that thought. Train your mind to detect immediately and instinctively what or who may be attempting to bring you down. When something is under your radar, you are more prone to identify and protect what is yours. So, suit up!

PRODUCTIVE PONDER

1. What are the negative things that you tell yourself?

   _____
   _____
   _____
   _____

2. How can you reframe those thoughts?

   _____
   _____
   _____
   _____

3. Who or what threatens your capacity to accomplish things?

   _____
   _____
   _____
   _____

4. How can you prepare yourself to address and demolish any posed threats?

_____

_____

_____

_____

Principle #2 – Don't Feel Accomplished By Mere Intentions

It is one thing to intend to do something; it is a completely different thing to actually do something. All too often, we think of and even communicate very good intentions about one thing or another, and we mean well but never quite get around to following through.

Let me put it to you this way: Good intentions never got the job done. You can intend all day long, but it does nothing for accomplishing your tasks or goals. You do not want to wake up one day and realize how much time has passed while you were busy intending to do things. You do not want to find yourself wishing you had promoted your words and thoughts to action.

Intention is a plan that you have written or committed to thought. Having a plan is fine; in fact, you will read later in this book that you should always create a plan. However, you must also be willing to *work* the plan. In order to achieve results, you must commit to action. Regardless of how many intentions you have or how long you've held out on them, the good thing is that, in most cases, you have an opportunity implement. Recognize your intents when they surface, determine whether it is something that you need to put into action, and get going now before it becomes a distant memory and possible regret.

PRODUCTIVE PONDER

1. What are some things that you have been intending on doing?

___

2. What tasks can you complete today from your response to number one?

___

3. How have your intentions delayed productivity in any aspect of your life or business?

___

Principle #3 – Distractions Are Like Contractions

When you begin to realize that distractions are only temporary, you become more patient with them. You begin to prepare yourself for distractions when outlining a plan of attack for your "to-dos" or goal achievement. Now, developing patience for distractions does not mean that you have to become best friends with things that pull you away from your plan; instead, it means that you are positioned to better deal with distractions.

Some of us are frazzled and thrown off our game at the mere sight of anything unplanned. While understanding that you cannot control everything, you must prepare for the unknown and the unexpected. You might ask: What is the point of having a plan if you are prone to distraction? The most important piece to your success is to stay on your set strategy, because that is your desired systematic approach to achieving your goal, completing a task, or working through your "to-do" list. The path to your goal serves as your road map and is there to get you back on course whenever life throws curve balls.

Just imagine, a mother carrying a child in her womb. Her ultimate goal is to deliver a healthy baby in nine months. During those months of carrying the baby, contractions occur, causing the mother to jump, groan, and feel pain. Though the contractions are temporary, they occur often. Despite the pain and distraction, the mother must continue carrying the baby to term. She probably will not cease the process just because she experienced contractions. She sticks with it until she reaches her goal, which is always worth enduring a few distractions for—well in this case contractions.

 **PRODUCTIVE PONDER**

1. What do you consider a distraction for you?

2. Why do you allow distractions to throw you off track toward your ultimate goal?

3. How can you better prepare your mind to deal with and bounce back from the distractions outlined in number one?

Principle #4 – Develop Rituals

The first three principles are the fundamental thoughts required to begin increasing your overall productivity while maintaining peace of mind. Now you must consider actions, because what you constantly do sets you up for what you always get in life. Think about the rituals that have shaped your current condition: Are they getting you unstuck in life and helping you get things done? If you are not bearing the fruit you desire then your rituals are not working.

A ritual is something that you do every day, usually at the same time each day, which creates the foundation for your days and ultimately your life. Many times, we live by rituals, often times not recognizing that those repeated actions could be the very thing that either propels or stagnates your ability to produce results. For this very reason, it is important to identify what habits you have created that may inhibit growth.

Do you find yourself going with the flow and playing each day by ear without any expectations? If so, this would mean that you always hop out of bed and hit the floor running with no concern for what the day holds or even what it is that you need to do. By implementing a simple ritual, setting aside a few minutes every morning to get clear about your goals and desires, you set the tone for the day. For instance, creating a list of "to-dos" or adding appointments to your calendar prior to starting your day can change your ability to consistently produce, achieve, and accomplish those things.

Your rituals, the habits that you have created, control you. Believe it or not, you already have rituals for your finances, relationships, career, and every other thing you manage in life. Whether you intentionally or unintentionally created the rituals, they are habits you now live by. It is up to you to determine if you need to make some changes to incorporate rituals that will get you closer to your goals in every aspect of life. Only *you* can make the transition.

💡 Productive Ponder

1. In what areas of life do you want to become more productive?

   _____

   _____

   _____

   _____

2. What rituals can you implement to increase overall productivity?

   _____

   _____

   _____

   _____

3. What time of the day, every day, can you implement the rituals listed in number two?

   _____

   _____

   _____

   _____

Principle #5 – Closed Mouths Don't Get Fed

We have all heard this phrase and perhaps you have even been told it: Closed mouths don't get fed. This applies to every person, regardless of his or her situation. If you want something, you must be confident and courageous enough to ask for it. Many are just afraid to ask for what they want or need, which keeps them stuck. To another end, while some are comfortable asking for what they deserve, they do not ask for what they are *worth*. Most are plagued by what others may think about them. Perhaps you are one of these people. You worry that "they" will not think you are good enough, you are weak for asking, or your request has no value. You worry about all possible negatives that then deter you from opening your mouth to say, "I need" or "I am worth."

In life, you carry many titles, duties, tasks, responsibilities, and requirements, but no one ever said that you must do it all on your own. So then, where did you adapt that mentality? Going at life alone only adds strife and strain on you physically, mentally, and spiritually—simply put it is draining. Self-inflicted stress is a sure sign of insufficient self-care.

If you know that you need assistance, expert advice, or anything else, it is time to open your mouth and communicate your needs to someone who can provide. Be sure to consider those who have your best interest at heart and will truly deliver. The last thing you need is to have someone agree to help, and you have the burden of needing to make sure the job is being done. More stress! Be very clear about your needs and know exactly who can fulfill your need. And never forget: You must always be willing to offer a hand up before asking for a hand out.

Once you ask for help, it is important to note that not all assistance is free of charge, so be prepared to compensate where necessary. I would much rather pay for help to relieve myself of an unnecessary burden than to continue carrying weight that holds me back from progressing in other areas of life. For instance, I convinced my husband to hire someone to clean our house. It took some time, but he finally agreed. We decided that she would only come once a month to help keep the house tidy. To our surprise, the expense was not as much as we thought it would be and that presented a relief in itself. The bigger win is that I am now able to redirect my focus on other tasks and duties that are more important like my family, business, and more. In essence, I was able to delegate a task that freed up time and created a clean space for my family to enjoy.

💡 Productive Ponder

1. What area of your life can you use help in?

   _____

   _____

   _____

   _____

2. Who can help you in those areas and how can you help them in return?

   _____

   _____

   _____

   _____

3. How are you going to ask for the help you need, and when will you ask for it?

   _____

   _____

   _____

   _____

Principle #6 – Do More Than Get It, Keep It

Some of us are persistent when it comes to getting what we want. Admit it, you will do whatever it takes to fulfill a desire of yours, right? When we are talking about something you feel that you must have or do in life, come Hell or high water, you are going to get it done and find the resources necessary to get you there.

Here is the most important question to ask once you obtain something (whatever this "something" is for you): How do you manage to keep it? You were persistent enough to achieve your goal, but if it is a goal that requires maintenance, you must have discipline. Consistency is vital to keeping what you have worked to obtain. In many cases, to grind for gain is much easier than to grind for keeps.

When talking about overall productivity, consistency is what makes the benefits truly manifest. By working with consistency, you build strength; whatever you spend the most time on is what determines how your hours, days, months, and years develop. What you committed to habit in the past is what laid the foundation for how your life is today (this idea ties back to the rituals discussed in Principle 4). The way you spend most of your time is a sneak peek into what your life will manifest. If you want to achieve a goal and create better, more successful habits, you must build the right muscles. Always consider the daily actions that will determine the course of your life.

Intentional Living

💡 Productive Ponder

1. What actions can you commit to everyday that will get you closer to your goals?

   _____

   _____

   _____

   _____

2. Create a schedule outlining each action, the day to perform, and the time. Use this to measure your progress and remain on track.

   _____

   _____

   _____

   _____

3. How will you make up for the days you missed to work towards your goals?

   _____

   _____

   _____

   _____

4. How do you plan to identify and change actions that you later determine are not in alignment with your goals?

_____
_____
_____
_____

Principle #7 – It's Hard to See the Picture When You Are In The Frame

The points discussed in these first seven principles require true dedication, will, determination, and consistency to incorporate into your life, especially if you have not done so before. It is an overall mindset shift that perhaps, prior to reading this book, you were not prepared to receive. Great! That means we are getting somewhere; you are beginning to see life through different lenses. Still, your new pair of specs does not necessarily mean that you now see everything about the process of increasing your productivity while maintaining a peace of mind. There is more to it and, as discussed in previous principles, you cannot always do it alone.

Imagine that you walk through life inside a picture frame. As you live your life, you may think everything is picture perfect from the inside looking out, but from someone on the outside looking in, there is a completely different view. You absolutely cannot view both perspectives of self, even when using a mirror. Having a coach, mentor, and accountability partner is crucial to learning more about yourself. Identify someone who you can trust to tell you the truth in a loving way.

Did you know that all of the greats have an advisor or trusted team of advisors? Even Oprah has coaches that she hires to guide her through various parts of her life. In fact, those who are serious about growing choose to go with a coach for the following reasons: 1) Coaches are experts in their fields, 2) they represent the view outside the frame, and 3) they are trained to guide, support, and inspire. While a mentor or accountability partner may be free of charge and thus temporarily beneficial, the investment you make with a viable coach offers a lifetime of change. When you invest in a coach, you own the time you paid for and the time is arranged exclusively to upgrade you in any area of your life.

Intentional Living

💡 PRODUCTIVE PONDER

1. Who do you have looking at your picture from the outside? What insight have you received thus far?

   _____

   _____

   _____

   _____

2. How do you think you would benefit from having an accountability partner, coach, or mentor?

   _____

   _____

   _____

   _____

3. What type of support do you feel you need most and why?

   _____

   _____

   _____

   _____

4. Who would you be interested in working with for the role identified in number three and how will you go about arranging a partnership?

_____

_____

_____

_____

DON'T FAIL TO PLAN

"Fail to plan then you plan to fail."

—Benjamin Franklin

Principle #8 – Ask The Right Questions

As a lifelong learner, I have been trained to ask the right questions in order to reach my intended goal. The truth is that the answer you receive is only as good as your question. With that being said, framing the proper question requires clarity around what it is that you seek to receive. Not only must your inquiry be clear to an outsider, but it must also be positioned to return a response that gets you closer to your destination.

In corporate America, I have both worked as an auditor and partnered with auditors. My goal was to become very familiar with the process under review so that I may obtain a clear understanding of what the business functions are and, most importantly, where issues might be prevalent. In order to be successful, it was pertinent that my team asked the right questions to the right people. There were times when we had to ask the wrong people in order to get to the right ones, but nevertheless, we were adamant about receiving answers.

Even when partnering with auditors, the requirements were the same. I was frequently asked to train associates on ways to best engage with auditors during a review. I placed great emphasis on asking questions for clarification whenever auditors posed an inquiry. This was necessary to ensure the proper contact was in place to answer and confirm an appropriate response.

What does all this mean? Well, just as with auditing to find gaps in a process, you must ask the right questions to fill the gaps in your life. To successfully achieve productivity, you need to be clear on what you need answers to and who has those answers. Above all, do not be afraid to ask. Fear will keep you spinning your wheels and wasting time as you try to figure it out alone—pure exhaustion with no results. You may even fear asking the wrong questions or people having a negative perception of you because of what you asked. As the saying goes, no question is a dumb question. It will cost you more to continue on in a misguided direction than to ask the wrong question to the wrong person. Who knows? You might find more clarity in exhausting all resources to arrive at an answer. So do it—ask away!

💡 Productive Ponder

1. What questions are you asking that relate to increasing your productivity?

_____

_____

_____

_____

2. Who are you posing the questions to and why?

_____

_____

_____

_____

3. What kind of response would you like? How can you achieve that result?

_____

_____

_____

_____

Principle #9 – Don't Reinvent The Wheel

There is nothing new under the sun. Most anything you do or decide to do has already been done by someone. You can certainly tweak the overall look and feel, and add your flavor to anything. In fact, I urge you to do just that. The challenge is that many procrastinate or veer away from being productive with their dreams and goals because they do not know how to start or where to begin. Better yet, they are discouraged because someone else is doing something similar.

You may be afraid to ask or perhaps you think you don't know anyone who is living your dream. If you are truly committed with your heart and soul, it is up to you to make the proper connections, release the fear, and rid preconceived notions. Whatever your goal or grand idea, more than likely someone else has already thought of it. Know that thinking and implementing are two completely different activities, so if someone had come up with your idea but has not yet implemented it, there is an opportunity for you to do it. If they have followed through, you still have many opportunities to make the idea even more innovative and unique to you.

Whether there is someone who has thought it or done it, you now have resources to leverage. Do not be so prideful that you would much rather figure it out all on your own. Going at it solo turns a month project into a year and a year into two. I don't know about you, but if there is an opportunity to achieve my goals easier and quicker, I am open to explore my options.

For some, leveraging available resources might be a scary thing, simply because they assume that it will cost them financially, and often times, this is true. Ask yourself how important it is for you to achieve this goal with as less stress as possible, and then do what it takes to get there. This could mean investing in a coach, attorney, or other expert to do a job or guide you through the process.

Productive Ponder

1. Describe how committed you are to implementing your ideas.

   _____
   _____
   _____
   _____

2. How are you willing to invest in you to get the information required for implementation?

   _____
   _____
   _____
   _____

3. Make a list of potential success partners who are equipped and experienced to provide you guidance.

   _____
   _____
   _____
   _____

4. Create a plan for reaching out to the contacts listed for number three. Then begin making calls, sending emails, or selecting whatever mode of communication is appropriate for the person you decide to connect with.

_____
_____
_____
_____

Principle #10 – Master One Task At A Time

I am a multi-tasker to the core. I am guilty of having multiple projects in flight at once and I do a good job managing all of them. However, here's what I learned about myself and how multi-tasking stifled my productivity early on: There are only certain tasks that I can effectively manage simultaneously, which leaves the others more neglected. I had to become clear about which activities and tasks fell into each category and manage accordingly. Understanding the challenges and level of focus needed to succeed is key.

In the early stages of business creation, I grew excited about the many ideas I had and instead of deciding on one to conquer, I started them all at once. Keep in mind that these were startups and I had no support team to assist with completing the many tasks required to get things up and running. With this approach, no one endeavor received my full attention, hence the businesses grew slowly and there was great strain on me, both mentally and physically.

One of my coaches had to reel me back, telling me that I could not "help but to do stuff," and she was right. Whether with my business or my personal life, I would juggle whatever to get my desired outcome. And here was my hang up: Whenever I learned something new, I wanted to quickly apply it. I mean, why wait? At least that had been my philosophy. However, I realized from my mistake and working with my coach that, if I was to derive the most promising return, my attention needed to be somewhere other than merely multitasking. I learned to become very aware of what activity would get me to my goal soonest and focus on that *one* task. Once the necessary task was completed and the goal achieved, I would then, and only then, move on to the next project. If you get really good at this, soon you will be knocking out projects like a pro.

Too many of us bite off more than we can chew, grow overwhelmed, and then simply give up on everything, because we feel like we failed. Do not confuse being overwhelmed with underachieving. As Sheryl Sandberg so eloquently stated in her book, *Lean In*, "Trying to do it all and expecting that it all can be done exactly right is a recipe for disappointment." It would be that much more beneficial for you and your life if you would choose to focus on one thing, master it, then move to the next.

 **PRODUCTIVE PONDER**

1. List all the major tasks or goals you are currently juggling.

   _____
   _____
   _____
   _____

2. What one task or goal can you pull from your list to focus on and complete in the next month?

   _____
   _____
   _____
   _____

3. Identify a task or goal per month that you can focus on and complete in a thirty-day period. Write each in the space below, specifying which month you plan to complete the goal.

   _____
   _____
   _____
   _____

4. Brainstorm ways to maintain your focus for each project and avoid getting off track. Document and refer back to this list as needed.

_____

_____

_____

_____

Principle #11 – Know Your "Why"

The thing that gets me going and keeps me going is family. Everything I do is to create a better life for those I love, from my husband and unborn child to my parents and beyond. Leaving a legacy is necessary and I will do whatever it takes to do so. Family is my "why" and my "what" is leaving a legacy. In essence, I created a habit of beginning with the end in mind.

I learned early in my success journey that being clear on your "why" is what carries you through to the finish line. Your "why" is that thing that gets you out of bed and into action when you are tired, sick, and worn out. Your "why" is so strong that you never concern yourself with "how;" instead, you have faith in knowing your focus on the "why" will figure out the "how." Stephen Covey, author of *The Seven Habits of Highly Effective People*, wrote, "To begin with the end in mind means to start with a clear understanding of your destination."

Do not waste time doing things just for the heck of it. You will never get those hours back. Many are committed to busy work, moving fast and constantly with no true motive. We often live too long without purpose, direction, or effective action, getting caught up in the rat race and hopping on the wheel as soon as we see an open seat. We don't know our destination, but we feel some sense of comfort in knowing that we are moving, even if it is in circles.

I encourage you to get off the wheel of busy work and

get clear about your destination and "why" you want to arrive there. Determine those things and the "how" will present itself.

Intentional Living

💡 Productive Ponder

1. What is your "why?"

_____

_____

_____

_____

2. Why is that your "why?" Elaborate on how your "why" motivates and encourages you.

_____

_____

_____

_____

3. What can you do now to move from how you've always done things to doing what's necessary for the sake of your "why?"

_____

_____

_____

_____

4. How can you position yourself to receive your "how?"

_____

_____

_____

_____

Principle #12 – There's Never A Perfect Moment

How many times have you postponed something that you wanted to do because you were waiting for the perfect moment? We all are guilty of doing this a time or two. You decided to wait until you paid all your bills off before attending college. You thought about starting a business but wanted to finish remodeling your home first. Because work had you so busy, you never wrote that book.

The truth is that, even when there is just one reason to wait, there will be another right after. In other words, there will always be an easy way out if you want it. People who are productive, effective, and successful get things done without concern for the "perfect time," because there is no such thing. Life happens to us all, and there is a chance that, when you decide to take action, other distractions will come up. It is imperative that you stay on course. Stop and tend to life matters if necessary, but never neglect your goals and dreams as long as you have breath in you.

As an implementer, I set my mind on something, research it, and then do it! I monitor the balance between phases, not spending too much time in any of them. It is your time to move from thinking to doing without concerns for the "right time." You want to end up in a position free of regrets and shoulda, woulda, couldas. Always remember there is never a perfect moment; instead, it is up to us to make the moments we have perfect.

Productive Ponder

1. What have you put off, waiting for the "perfect time?"

\
\
\
\

2. Your perfect time is now, so what is it that you are going to put into action?

\
\
\
\

3. What are you afraid of when it comes to achieving your goals and making your dreams come true?

\
\
\
\

4. Why are you afraid? What's the worst that could happen?

_____
_____
_____
_____

Principle #13 – Fail To Plan, Plan To Fail

"If you fail to plan, then you plan to fail." The first time I heard this phrase was when I was a teenager. I sat in the pews of a church with several other teens during vacation bible school. One of the youth ministers spoke to us about setting goals, attending college, and having a life plan. Since that day, I have always reminded myself to not only plan, but also to actually implement those plans in all aspects of life.

Going about your days without a plan is like driving to an unfamiliar location without a roadmap (or these days a navigation application). You wander blindly with no sense of direction or awareness of milestones to signify how near or far you are. It is important to know your destination so that, in your plan, you are able to approach it with appropriate sub-steps, which will be your day-to-day focus. Not only does this prepare you for what's next, but it also illustrates a big picture view of your goal while also giving you incentives for each day.

Know that not everything will go as planned—life happens. The benefit of having a plan is that, when you get off track, you are able to pick up where you left off. You can always adjust, make changes, add, or subtract. We evolve and so do our life goals, ambitions, and desires.

Now that you created a mindset shift and a plan, you are set to move on to the next level of maximizing your time and increasing productivity.

💡 Productive Ponder

1. In what aspects of your life do you have a well thought-out plan? If none, begin documenting one.

   _____
   _____
   _____
   _____

2. If you do not have a plan, why not?

   _____
   _____
   _____
   _____

3. How would a written plan change how you approach your days?

   _____
   _____
   _____
   _____

4. How has going about your days haphazardly pushed you closer to your overall goal?

_____

_____

_____

_____

MAKE EVERY MINUTE COUNT

"In every day, there are 1,440 minutes. That means we have 1,440 daily opportunities to make a positive impact."

—Les Brown

Principle #14 – Maintain A Trusted System

In order to keep track of and measure your success, you must create a trusted system. A trusted system has two parts: 1) A centralized location for all your notes, documentation of your goals, overall plan, and anything else related to your productivity, and 2) a location that is sacred because it is your go-to for all things action related. For some, a trusted system may be a calendar book, notebook, or folder maintained on a daily basis and stored in a place where it is visible, or at least accessible, at all times.

Within this trusted system is your full life plan, business goals, or professional endeavors with carefully outlined milestones, deadlines, and all other information that help monitor progress. It is always nice to have a written plan of what you want to accomplish and when. It is key to have a constant reminder of the activities requiring completion and how they lead up to your ultimate goal! I personally like to write tasks on a calendar—it is my trusted system and goes wherever I go. You may prefer an electronic form of tracking or both. Whatever method best suits your lifestyle is what you should go with.

Wondering why this principle has any importance? It's simple: The more you see your goals, the more likely you are to remember and to act. In essence, your preferred trusted system will become your best friend. Constantly refer to it and update it. Pay close attention to measurable tasks so that you are able to quickly identify where you are off track or perhaps even ahead of schedule.

💡 Productive Ponder

1. How would a trusted system change how you go about life?

   _____

   _____

   _____

   _____

2. Where is the best place for your trusted system (i.e. diary, notebook, calendar, etc.)? Why?

   _____

   _____

   _____

   _____

3. How do you plan to systematize your progress on tasks using a trusted system?

   _____

   _____

   _____

   _____

Principle #15 – Timing Is Everything

If something is meant to be, there is no need to rush. It will happen in the right time, with the right person, for the right reason. Think about your past. You can probably agree that things always manifest when you are prepared to receive it. If you cannot attest to that statement, it is probably because you did not commit to the work you should have while awaiting fruition. Cutting to the crux of it all, there is a season for planting and then there is a season for reaping. Know which season you are in and act accordingly.

Your season could vary for different areas of life. For instance, while you could be sowing in your business, you could be reaping benefits from your health routine. On the other hand, your career may have already taken off as you so desired, but you are now planting seeds of wisdom for your spirituality. Everything and everyone has a divine time to blossom and show up as whom or what it was meant to be. Just as a caterpillar experiences the process of metamorphosis in order to evolve into a butterfly, so will every aspect of your life transform. There is no getting around this.

Once you realize and accept this process, you will progress through life with much more ease and peace of mind. Understanding that timing is everything, you can focus on the now and do what it takes to achieve your desired future state. Those who are truly committed are consistent and dedicated. People who make sacrifices now that most others don't will find themselves later living a life that most others don't.

Intentional Living

💡 Productive Ponder

1. Why are you in such a hurry if what is meant for you will eventually be?

   _____

   _____

   _____

   _____

2. How are you going to be productive now in order to reap benefits in the future?

   _____

   _____

   _____

   _____

3. Which areas of life are you sowing and which are you reaping? Explain.

   _____

   _____

   _____

   _____

Principle #16 – Devote Time

Everyone has a time of the day during which he or she is most productive. Are you a morning person? Do you beat the sun and rise with energy to go about your day? Or are you an afternoon person? Do you get going after a few cups of coffee, quiet time, and reading the newspaper? Maybe you are a night owl, staying up and grinding into the wee hours of the morning.

Of course, there are folks that fall somewhere in-between those categories. What matters most is that you are aware of your most productive pockets of time so that you are able to take full advantage of that stretch. With a pre-outlined plan, you are always able to jump right in and tackle the necessary tasks when your productivity pocket hits. There will be no guessing, no wasting time, and no going with the flow.

To decrease the number of distractions during your devoted time, it is important to choose a sacred space where you are less likely to receive interruptions. According to David Allen, author of *Getting Things Done*, "If your space is properly set up and streamlined, it can reduce your unconscious resistance to dealing with [getting things done] and even make it attractive for you to sit down and crank through your work." Because many of us have responsibilities to others, it is pertinent that you set boundaries and expectations with everyone around you. Do not feel guilty for setting aside time for yourself to get things done or to reground. If you desire accomplishment and success, there will be sacrifices to make and changes that not only you, but also those who love you, will have to adjust to.

 **Productive Ponder**

1. What times of the day are you most alert, energetic, and eager to do things?

   _____
   _____
   _____
   _____

2. What will it take for you to regularly set aside time and commit to using that time to work on your goals?

   _____
   _____
   _____
   _____

3. How can you take advantage of your productive pocket of time?

   _____
   _____
   _____
   _____

Principle #17 – Low-Hanging Fruit

At this point, you now understand the importance of having clarity, a documented plan, a trusted system, and being prepared. Once you are sitting in your productive pocket of time gazing at your plan, you might ask "Now what?" We all do it—even when a plan is laid out, you wonder where to start. It is a natural state of nervousness, especially when you are just getting started with this productivity thing.

If you have ever stood under a tree bearing fruit, you know that it is easiest to grab what is hanging low. It is accessible and does not cause much strain or too many steps to retrieve. In tackling your daily tasks and chipping away at your ever-growing "to-do" list, consider the same approach. Ask yourself what items on your list will take ten minutes or less to complete—those are what you would label as your "low-hanging fruit." Once you are clear as to what those tasks are, knock them out. Get them done and mark them off your list. I promise you will notice an immediate relief.

Many set aside quick and easy tasks for last because they believe that those menial duties can wait; after all, the completion process will take no time. In this approach, you begin tackling bigger, more time-consuming tasks that could possible carry on for hours or days, causing you to feel unproductive. Remember, if you spend time on the larger tasks first, it will take longer for you to check things off your list. Instead, try picking off the low-hanging fruit and jump-starting your productivity.

Intentional Living

💡 Productive Ponder

1. Which of your daily tasks are low-hanging fruits?

   _____

   _____

   _____

   _____

2. Commit to working on low-hanging fruit tasks first. Explain how you will begin and complete the tasks listed in number one.

   _____

   _____

   _____

   _____

3. How can prioritizing completion of less time-consuming tasks increase your productivity?

   _____

   _____

   _____

   _____

Principle #18 – You Touch It, You Finish It

Have you been in a store with delicate and expensive items, all protected with signs strategically reading, "*Do not touch?*" Let us go a step further: Have you ever heard a shopkeeper say, "You break it, you buy it?" In so many ways, those words alone create a fear of touching that thing, so you don't, unless you know for sure that you are going to make a purchase.

Think of your "to-do" list as that store with an inventory of delicate items available for purchase. Except in this case, no lurking allowed. This is all "You touch it, you buy it." What does this mean? Anything that you start on your "to-do" list, you *must* finish. Following through is essential to productivity. All too often, we start one project or task, never finish it, and then pick up a new task. If you continue that cycle, you will create a calamity of many open tasks and none ready to mark "complete." Can you imagine how stagnant you will feel and how overwhelmed you will increasingly become?

Do yourself a favor and only start what you plan to finish and always finish what you start. Creating such a mindset will lay the foundation for your ability to carry tasks through to the end. Remember that this too is a process and you must create a habit that will change the way you approach your daily tasks and goals forever.

Intentional Living

💡 Productive Ponder

1. Do you often leave tasks incomplete and prematurely move to the next? What do you think causes you to start multiple tasks at once?

_____

_____

_____

_____

2. How many tasks do you have in progress now and what are they?

_____

_____

_____

_____

3. Which of those "in-progress" projects can you focus on and complete in one day? Designate a day per task and commit to finishing each.

_____

_____

_____

_____

4. What can you do in the future to focus on completing one major task prior to starting a new one?

_____

_____

_____

_____

MAKE IT HAPPEN

"The way to get started is to quit talking and begin doing."

—Walt Disney

Principle #19 – Documentation Beats Conversation

In the past six years, I've had four laptops, all PCs prior to my current Apple device. None of those past four times did I upgrade or purchase the newest laptop just for the sake of having the most advanced gadget. No, each system crashed at the most important times. But honestly, when you rely on your computer daily, when is it ever a good time to deal with a sick laptop?

The first time my laptop went caput, I was like an infant throwing a tantrum at the loss of her pacifier. I truly lost it! Pun intended—I lost data and my mind. What makes matters worse is that, during one of the technological breakdowns, I was in the midst of my doctoral studies and all of my blood, sweat, and tears were stored on my laptop. It goes without saying that it was in that moment I realized the importance of an external hard drive and backing up data.

All too often, we do the same with our brains. We continue to pile loads of information in our minds, hoping that all of it will stick and that we will remember everything. That is, of course, until the epic fail: You forget something very important and it changes everything #SystemCrash. It comes down to the fact that our brains are simply not designed to remember everything. In fact, our brains deliberately make us forget things to prevent insanity. In essence, if you are not frequently performing a brain data dump and documenting your thoughts, you can almost expect a crash to happen at any moment!

Although there is no external hard drive we can plug into our brains, we do have the ability to get those many thoughts out of our minds and onto paper. Research has proven that people remember 10 percent of what they read, 20 percent of what they hear, 30 percent of what they see, and 70 percent of what they say and write (Thalheimer, 2015). Therefore, kudos to you for thinking and saying it, but now it is time to write it all down.

Productive Ponder

1. How can documenting your plan, actions, and intentions improve your follow through?

   _____
   _____
   _____
   _____

2. What can you do differently to incorporate a habit of documenting your plans and thoughts?

   _____
   _____
   _____
   _____

3. How would documenting tasks and events change your life?

   _____
   _____
   _____
   _____

Intentional Living

4. How can you position yourself to better control and remember the important things in life?

_____

_____

_____

_____

Principle #20 – Clarity Is King

How does uncertainty and obscurity exists in your life? Just imagine getting through everyday with blurred vision or a sheet of fog clouding your view so much that you are stumbling, making wrong turns, falling, and bumping into people and things. Can you fathom how clumsy you would look or how dangerous such a situation could be?

That is exactly how many of us walk through life, unclear about where we are going and letting our days run us instead of taking control of our days. We go about aimlessly, expecting great things to happen while "going with the flow." But where is the "flow" leading you? Is it to the place you desire to be in your life, profession, or business?

In order to know if you are, every day, moving closer to your desired state, you must know where it is you want to go. Get clear about your goals, ambitions, and dreams. Sit with yourself and determine exactly what it is you want out of life. It is not important to take any actions in this step; instead, what bears the most importance is connecting with your "Why," your purpose.

I know that finding clarity is a touchy subject, because so many of us struggle to identify our purpose or goals. But in many cases, your purpose is starring you in the face every day, just waiting on you to realize its significance to you and your life. Pay attention to those things you do effortlessly, things others consistently compliment you on, and things you literally lose track of time while doing. There, you will find hidden treasures.

💡 Productive Ponder

1. What do you want to accomplish in your life, profession, or business?

   _____
   _____
   _____
   _____

2. Does what you want to accomplish make you smile inside and out? If so, why? If not, what does?

   _____
   _____
   _____
   _____

3. What are the tasks that will help you achieve your desired outcomes in life?

   _____
   _____
   _____
   _____

4. Now that you are committed to doing the work, how will you go about gaining clarity on your goals?

_____

_____

_____

_____

Principle #21 – Slow It Down To Break it Down

We live in such a fast-paced world—everyone is on the go and always rushing. Most have very little patience with anything or anyone, including themselves. For some strange reason, a majority of the world's population is under the inaccurate impression that, because there is desire, the desired thing (whatever you want manifested in your life) should magically appear when they want it. Somewhere along the way, they forget that success takes time, dedication, will, consistency, and patience.

It takes approximately four weeks for you to notice a change, eight for your friends to notice, and twelve for the rest of the world to notice. In other words, it takes time for things to evolve into what we envision. Furthermore, as your mindset matures, you will begin to realize that change actually occurs well before you see it—that is, if you are considering all possible perspectives. In his book *Outliers,* Malcolm Gladwell explains that, in order to become an expert, one must commit to 10000 hours performing or practicing a single skill. If this is in fact true, that is just over 416 days: A full year (all day, everyday) plus some.

The 10000-hour philosophy can be daunting. However the point is, it takes time for people and things to develop and it is not always in our timing. Often, when you take your time and enjoy the process, time flies and you look up to find all that you imagined manifesting. Rushing through the process causes you to miss some of the greatest lessons, relationships, and opportunities; however, when you allow nature to take its course, you decrease your chances of being overwhelmed, stressed, and strained. Enjoy the ride and appreciate how beautifully *your* process grows!

💡 Productive Ponder

1. What opportunities have you missed by rushing through life?

   _____
   _____
   _____
   _____

2. How much unnecessary strain and strife have you caused yourself as a result of feeling behind in life?

   _____
   _____
   _____
   _____

3. How would life be different if you embraced the thought that you are right where you should be at this time?

   _____
   _____
   _____
   _____

Principle #22 – Organize, Don't Agonize

Is your lack of organization causing you mental and physical agony? Do you realize that disorganization can apply to both your mental state and the tangible things in your life? Have you ever considered that the mess you live in reflects your life in general?

If your living quarter is always in disarray, it is no wonder you are late everywhere you go or that you can never find something when you need it. You live in a catastrophe! Physical clutter spills over into how you work and play in life. In January of 2011, Princeton University's Neuroscience Institute published an article discussing the relation between cluttered environments and one's mental focus. The study proved that physical disarray and disorganization causes focus loss, depression, anxiety, and somberness. Imagine how those feelings would affect your mindset and outlook on life. You would begin to feel defeated and exhausted, causing your mind to tell your body not to move. That's when you succumb to the unproductive spell.

Whether you experience disorganization in a physical sense or not, mental clutter can still arise. When you have so many tasks, commitments, chores, and other commotions running through your mind, it is just as taxing as physical clutter. If you commit too much information to memory, you will grow overwhelmed and it will show: Forgetting important tasks, taking last minute actions, having repeated tardiness, and continually disappointing yourself and others. Eventually such activities will weigh heavy on your mental and physical state.

So de-clutter your space and your mind! Begin with one room at a time and dispose of things you have not used in the last year. File or shred all paperwork. Find creative ways to store things in closets so that it is easily accessible and neat. Strategically place items where you will remember exactly where to go when needed.

If you are reading this thinking, "Gosh, that is yet another thing to do," then you have it all wrong. This one more thing will change the course of your journey and significantly improve your productivity. Set aside some time to straighten out your space, physically and mentally!

💡 Productive Ponder

1. How much peace could you gain by setting aside time to de-clutter your mind and your space?

_____

_____

_____

_____

2. If you became organized, what would be different about your physical space or mental state?

_____

_____

_____

_____

3. Why are you procrastinating on doing things that will completely shift your mindset?

_____

_____

_____

_____

Principle #23 – Schedule Your Priorities

There is a significant difference between what is urgent and what is important. The two are often confused when determining what to do or say first. While there should be a good reason for doing anything, some are caught up in doing a task or habit just because it has always been done. In order to resolve this, ask yourself early and often, "Why am I doing this?" That question alone will put things into perspective and perhaps even help determine what you should start, stop, and continue doing.

Upon confirming what actions or tasks you should continue, determine the items on your to-do list that are priority and those that are urgent: Priority items are those that are of high importance and give you the biggest payoff, while urgent items are those that are critical as it relates to time. Have clarity and focus while going through this undertaking.

To maximize your time, gain the most significant return by focusing on those items that are both priority and urgent first. Here are some rules of thumb to follow as Strong shared in her article, "Why Urgent is Not Priority:"

- If something is important and urgent, accomplish it now.

- If something is urgent but not important, try to avoid it.

- If something is important but not urgent, plan for it and get it done.

- If something is neither important nor urgent, skip it. Why waste your time?

Categorize each of your daily tasks as priority, urgent, or both and simply refer to the above rules to determine what you put into action first.

 **PRODUCTIVE PONDER**

1. To which tasks have you committed the majority of your time?

   _____
   _____
   _____
   _____

2. Of the tasks listed above, which are urgent and which are priority?

   _____
   _____
   _____
   _____

3. Have you been wasting your time on irrelevant tasks or things that you could easily delegate and free up time to complete priority tasks? Why?

   _____
   _____
   _____
   _____

Principle #24 – Align Your Tongues

I first heard this phrase while listening to a webinar. One of the feature speakers said to the audience, "Align the tongue in your mouth with the tongue in your shoe." In essence, what she was saying was "Stop talking about it. Be about it."

We are so often caught up in saying what we are going to do that some of us have tricked ourselves into believing that saying is doing. In some cases, this kind of talk can even attract attention and praise; in most cases, no one will call you on your bluff, particularly if leaving the task undone does not affect them.

But when implementation fails, excuses rear their ugly heads. Instead of admitting that it was just talk, we blame everything and everybody under the sun for that goal or task remaining unaccomplished. What holds true is that when you want something bad enough, you will find a way to get it. If you don't, you will find excuses. Which will you choose?

It's time to only speak what you truly plan to implement, because empty words get you nowhere. What's worse is that you will disappoint the most important person in your life: Yourself.

Intentional Living

💡 Productive Ponder

1. What are some things you said you would do but have not yet delivered on?

   _____

   _____

   _____

   _____

2. How can you make good on your promises and commitments moving forward?

   _____

   _____

   _____

   _____

3. Who can you depend on to hold you to your word? When will you ask them to hold you accountable?

   _____

   _____

   _____

   _____

4. Who do you need to apologize to for not following through on a task? Make the apology.

_____

_____

_____

_____

REFILL YOUR TANK

"I give up freely what is no longer serving me. I release it to create space for what inspires me."

—Iyanla VanZant

Principle #25 – When You Grow Tired, Rest, Don't Quit

Taking on too many tasks and responsibilities can be taxing on the mind and body. Sometimes, you just plain overdo it without realizing it until your body tells you so. While doing and going is not a bad thing, forgoing the balance between work and play is unhealthy.

Life takes us in a whirlwind most days. Our normal daily responsibilities are enough, let alone all the other things we commit to. You probably find yourself often thinking that there is never enough time to do all the things you need to and no time to do what you want. You are purely disregarding your health when you continue to push day after day without resting. At that rate, your body will eventually shut down and force you to rest, and if you are lucky, the shutdown will be something minor. But when your body is really upset with how you have neglected it, the results could very well be something critical.

Think about the frog in hot water story: A frog is placed into a pot of boiling water and immediately jumps out in reaction to the extreme temperature. However, when the same frog is placed into room temperature water that is gradually brought to a boil, he never jumps out and dies. You see, the frog in the second scenario adjusted to the temperature, but after giving off large amounts of energy for a duration of time to survive the situation, the frog eventually died.

Some of you are the frog in boiling water, continually giving energy to things that no longer serve you, just because you have always done it or because someone expects you to. Instead, consider what it means to your livelihood to continue pouring out without refilling your energy tank. Balancing work and play is the most important way to be productive. Pay attention to the early signs of overexertion and take a break. Remember, you only get one body: Refuel your energy, reignite your passion, and realign your actions with your ultimate goals.

💡 Productive Ponder

1. In which areas of life are you overexerting yourself?

   _____

   _____

   _____

   _____

2. Identify the responses in number one that are activities you enjoy doing and not something you do out of obligation. How can you delegate or remove those tasks that you do not enjoy or are not an expert at?

   _____

   _____

   _____

   _____

3. How can you better balance time for work and time for refueling?

   _____

   _____

   _____

   _____

4. Are you the frog that immediately jumps for safety (rest) when you are tired or do you sit in the boiling water (continue to push) until you are forced to rest? How has it helped or hurt you?

_____
_____
_____
_____

Principle #26 – Family First, No Exceptions

Even while you are on your grind, you must nurture important relationships that provide you laughter, love, invigoration and a safe haven. Do not get so busy that you have no time for those you love. In the end, they are the ones who support you in all your endeavors. That goes a long way and it is important that you reciprocate your appreciation.

When I get excited about a project, it is easy for me to dive in hard and deep. For this reason I had to train myself to not lose sight of what's most important to me and to create the habit of intentionally planning and scheduling time with family. Now, family may not always understand why you have not spent as much time with them and it's okay to set expectations so that everyone is on the same page. Furthermore, keep in mind that some family members or relatives do not require that level of insight—it is up to you to determine who does and who does not. But, without a doubt, those closest to you should be aware so that when you have to pull away and plug into "getting things done," all remains well in your household.

Remember that family is what sustains you and many of them are there when you need them. Remain unapologetic about your plans and continue to strategically push through, but don't wait until you need your family to express your love and spend time. Who knows? Someone may be willing to take some of the load off your plate, but to do that, they first need to know what's on your plate.

Productive Ponder

1. How can you find more time in your schedule with those you love? What are you going to do to ensure that you are not putting your family last on your priority list while you commit to achieving personal goals?

   _____
   _____
   _____
   _____

2. Create a plan to communicate to your family your endeavors and the requirements to achieve them. Specify when, how, who, and what.

   _____
   _____
   _____
   _____

3. Which days are designated for work and which are reserved for play? How will you hold yourself to this schedule?

_____

_____

_____

_____

4. Are you in communication with your immediate family so that your home remains a safe haven? How do you plan to keep the lines of communication open?

_____

_____

_____

_____

Principle #27 – Dedication To Meditation

Many people confuse meditation with prayer and do not understand the difference between the two. The best explanation that I have heard is that prayer is when you ask of and thank God, whereas meditation is when you listen for the answers. Powerful, right?

Meditation is yet another way to step away, clear your mind, and recall your purpose while withstanding this busy world—it's both energizing and renewing. Moreover, if you have patience, you will find that meditation is also inspiring. As the late Dr. Wayne Dyer eloquently explained, to be inspired means to be in spirit or connected to something greater than you. Meditation exalts you to that higher height.

Meditation is also time you reserve to be alone and reconnect with your spirit. Everyone has his or her varying approaches to meditation; it is truly, what works best for you. Some may recite a chant while others rotate a string of beads between their fingers to maintain focus. Some meditate with soft music while others prefer silence. Further, some prefer sitting upright while others opt to lie down. When I initially began meditating, I would fall asleep each time. With that experience, I quickly learned that I could not perform this exercise lying down and I could not commit to long periods. Paying attention to what works and what does not will better assist with developing your meditation muscle. Again, implement whatever works best for setting the most effective ambiance to keep you awake and grounded.

If you are a meditation newbie, I would suggest that you create your own mantra to read repeatedly during your meditation until you train your mind to focus. You will eventually be able to sit still with your mind and body and just listen. Meditation is a necessity especially if you are always on the go or have numerous responsibilities. Create a habit that will position you to realize ideas and thoughts you would have otherwise ignored, overlooked, or just plain missed. Stick with it: Incorporate a few days a week in small increments of time and gradually progress into a daily routine. You can do it!

💡 Productive Ponder

1. How do you think meditation will change your days?

   _____
   _____
   _____
   _____

2. Decide what times work best for you to begin incorporating a meditation routine. Get specific: Name the days of the week, time, and duration.

   _____
   _____
   _____
   _____

3. Create your very own mantra to recite during meditation. Write your mantra in the space below and read it during your meditation sessions to maintain focus.

   _____
   _____
   _____
   _____

Principle #28 – Know Your Limit

We talked about making family first and remaining in communication with those you love. This principle will cover how to engage those who are not family, but require your time as well. Whether personal or business, there will always be people and things demanding your attention. First things first: Stop over-committing! Just because you have always been in a particular role or you think no one else will take it on does not mean it will not survive without you.

Often times, people get stuck doing things that no longer serve them and begin to hate the very thing that previously brought them joy. You do not want to be the reason you despise an organization or activity. Know when it is time to move on to bigger and better things. That doesn't necessarily mean that you must discontinue involvement altogether; instead, try taking just a few steps back. Assess the entire matter so that you are able to make informed decisions.

Time is precious—it is important that you don't always find yourself giving it away to things that do not align with the legacy you intend to leave. When you understand this, your outlook on time management will completely shift: You will be able to reassess the activities that consumed a significant amount of your hours and determine if your tasks or involvement in organizations align with your goals. It was this very exercise that helped me realize that there were many things I needed to cease and desist. I then appropriately closed out involvement where determined necessary, which meant that I had to communicate carefully and honestly with people I worked with. I set boundaries to utilize my time productively and in line with my goals.

Not everyone will be happy for you nor will they all agree, but in the end, what matters is that you are satisfied with your decisions. As long as your actions align with your personal endeavors, you will ultimately achieve your goals and remain productive.

💡 Productive Ponder

1. What ties do you need to sever to increase productivity in areas that align with your ultimate goals?

   _____
   _____
   _____
   _____

2. How can you prepare extended family and friends for your transition out of the roles and responsibilities that no longer serve you?

   _____
   _____
   _____
   _____

3. When you set boundaries, some may support you while others disagree. How will you deal with the various responses from others?

   _____
   _____
   _____
   _____

Intentional Living

4. How will you ensure that, going forward, you only commit to things that align with your goals?

_____

_____

_____

_____

Principle #29 – Be Open To Change

Dr. Wayne Dyer often said, "Have a mind that's closed to nothing and open to everything." In life and business, we do not have all the answers, and if you think you do, you will find yourself stagnant. We must remain open to insight from others and the experiences we incur—that is the only way to grow. It is no different when desiring to increase overall productivity: Sometimes, it is imperative to change the way we think, see, and do things.

Many are accustomed to the way they have always done things and refuse to make any changes. This inflexibility causes many to grow unproductive. Productive individuals embody an open mind and willingness to adjust as necessary to make things happen. There may even be times when you begin in a certain direction and learn of a more efficient route after making what you thought was a significant amount of headway. It is absolutely okay to reassess and redirect. This re-evaluation does not imply that you failed; it simply shows maturity in your walk.

People also often dread the mere thought of change, viewing it as uncomfortable, unpredictable, and unsettling. When you think about it, doing the same thing aimlessly can also be described by those three adjectives. In fact, doing the same thing and expecting different results is insanity! If what you're doing is not working, it's indeed time to explore other avenues.

If you feel stuck, connect with someone who has already accomplished the very thing that you would like to achieve and pick their brains about ways you can get on the right track. As mentioned in an earlier principle, there is nothing new under the sun; As soon as you understand that, you will stop wasting time and begin joining forces for the better with someone who has been there and done that. There is no better time than now to hook your wagon onto another that is moving toward your destination and at the pace you desire. Just don't always expect to be pulled!

💡 Productive Ponder

1. What is that thing you have always done that is holding you back from progressing in your life or business?

   _____
   _____
   _____
   _____

2. How does continuing the action identified in number one serve you in your current state?

   _____
   _____
   _____
   _____

3. How will you overcome the fear of change to avoid any further delay in your overall achievements?

   _____
   _____
   _____
   _____

4. What can you redirect your actions and attention to that will get you closer to your goals?

_____
_____
_____
_____

Principle #30 – Celebrate Wins

It took some time for me to realize the importance of celebrating my accomplishments. Before, I would find myself achieving goals and immediately turning my focus to the next mission. I never basked in the greatness of completing a task or achieving a goal. These habits quickly created overwhelming frustration and I had to reckon with my inability to be satisfied with what I did, no matter how small or big. While setting goals seemed like a great idea, after doing the work and finally achieving, my mindset was always to undermine my accomplishments.

There is no stress that is beneficial to your health and it is especially detrimental when the stress is self-inflicted. Often times, we are hard on ourselves because of the influence we have on others or because we feel like we are running out of time; we simply want better for our family and ourselves. What I had to realize is that stressing only caused me to lose energy and grow ill, which, in turn, meant that I was incapable of being as productive as I normally would be. That is when my mindset shifted from the desire to constantly grind to taking moments to be thankful for every accomplishment.

My husband and I implemented a tool to help us recall all of our accomplishments from the year. It is simply a jar decorated with our names and a few other inspirational pictures and words. Each time either one of us has a win, achieve a planned goal, or go beyond our original plan, we write it down on a piece of paper and place it inside the jar. At the beginning of the New Year, we are going to open the jar and read every slip of paper to reminisce on all that we have accomplished as a family. This exercise not only helps us recall all of our wins, but also reminds us of all that we have to celebrate for the full year. We also celebrate as the wins occur.

I continue to create activities and tools that force me to celebrate every win. Without doing so, it is easy to become worn out and quickly feel under-accomplished as you strive for the next thing. Moving swiftly through your goals is good until you lose sight of how important what you have already done is. Therefore, I encourage you to take time to smell the roses: Realize how far you have come and pat yourself on the back, treat yourself to dinner, or share your accomplishment with others—do whatever honors the productive powerhouse that you are.

💡 Productive Ponder

1. What tool(s) can you incorporate in your day-to-day that will encourage celebrating your wins? How do you plan to use the tools listed?

   _____

   _____

   _____

   _____

2. Who can you partner up with to celebrate one another's wins? Identify celebration milestones and how you plan to celebrate each.

   _____

   _____

   _____

   _____

3. How will you remind yourself to take the time to recognize your accomplishments as they occur?

   _____

   _____

   _____

   _____

Conclusion

If you are reading this conclusion, you made it to the finish line. Congratulations on sticking with the process! That is a true sign that you are committed to making the necessary changes in your day-to-day life in order to win. You have already made the first step toward achieving your goals, moving beyond fear, creating the life you desire, and making moves that you for far too long have procrastinated on. The true challenge begins now, *after* you have been equipped with tools that will allow you to accept the leading role in your life.

To summarize, we discussed the following:

- Shift Your Mindset: Change your mind about what you can accomplish and realize that you are equipped to do anything. You must believe in you before anyone else can.

- Don't Fail to Plan: A clearly documented plan is important in keeping you honest, reminding you of your goals, and monitoring measurable outcomes.

- Make Every Minute Count: We all have the same twenty-four hours to take on our many responsibilities in life. It is up to you to account for each minute and use the time you have to achieve goals.

- Make it Happen: Stop talking about it and be about it. Implement the many thoughts and dreams you have held on to. Do what needs to be done to manifest a better future.

- <u>Refill Your Tank</u>: Take the time necessary to re-ground. Always strive to give from the best of you, not the stress in you, and commit to granting yourself regular times to re-energize and refresh.

I know this is a significant amount of information to digest; however, all these points are relevant to your success and feasible to incorporate into your life. I hope that you will regularly refer to this information as you continue your life's journey. Reflect on the questions at different points in your life to measure your growth and make sure you share your knowledge with your friends and family.

Remember, on the other side of fear is your dream and you are already massively empowered to achieve anything your heart desires. So get out of your own way!

About the Author

Dr. Jatun Dorsey is a mentor, speaker, certified life/business coach, professor, and Amazon best-selling author. She is passionate about influencing change and encouraging others to stand boldly in achieving personal goals. She teaches individuals who are jaded, overwhelmed, and overloaded on ways to do more of what invigorates and refreshes them. She gets to the core of her clients to help them gain clarity, ignite their passion, and authentically show up in life.

Dr. Jatun is a sought-after speaker who has delivered numerous presentations to women and professionals. Her down-to-earth approach captivates audiences while motivating them to be progressive towards their goals, make time for themselves, and increase overall productivity. She speaks at workshops, seminars, and conferences for corporations, organizations, institutions, and churches. With both a master's and doctorate in business administration, she supplements her lived experiences with structured knowledge. This combination has proven to be what her clients and audiences appreciate most about her methods of encouragement and motivation.

Dr. Jatun is also the founder of The Commend Her Network (TCHN), which is a 501(c)(3) organization that focuses on partnering with local women's shelters to support and position underprivileged women to regain confidence and re-enter the workforce. Since 2014, TCHN has been dedicated to encouraging all women to be in compliment instead of competition for connections and collaborative growth.

Her first book, *Fabulous New Life*, co-authored with twenty-seven other authors, reached Amazon's bestseller list in 2015. *Fabulous New Life* shares stories of experiencing life's challenges, heartbreaks, and disappointments, and illustrates how to come out bigger and better.

When not focusing on her passion of inspiring and encouraging others, Dr. Jatun enjoys spending time with family, dancing, relaxing, and singing karaoke. Her favorite things are massages, plum wine, laughter, and dates with her husband.

To connect with Dr. Jatun Dorsey, visit her website at www.drjatun.com

References

David Allen, *Getting Things Done: The Are of Stress-Free Productivity* (New York: Penguin, 2001), 87.

Stephen Covey, *The 7 Habits of Highly Effective People: Powerful Lessons in Personal Change* (New York: Free Press, 2003), 98.

Erin Doland, "Scientist Find Physical Clutter Negatively Affects Your Ability to Focus and Process Information," *The Journal of Neuroscience* (2011): accessed September 9, 2016, https://unclutterer.com/2011/03/29/scientists-find-physical-clutter-negatively-affects-your-ability-to-focus-process-information/.

Malcolm Gladwell, *Outliers: The Story of Success* (New York: Little, Brown and Company, 2008), 35-68.

Sheryl Sandberg, *Lean In: Women, Work, and The Will to Lead* (New York: Alfred A. Knopf, 2014), 123.

Laura Strong, "Why 'Urgent' is Not Priority: How to Keep Urgent But Not Important Tasks from Taking Over Your Day," Inc.com (2012): accessed September 9, 2016, http://www.inc.com/laura-strong/why-urgent-is-not-important.html.

Will Thalheimer, "Debunk This: People Remember 10 Percent of What They Read," Association for Talent Development (2015): accessed August 27, 2016, https://www.td.org/Publications/Blogs/Science-of-Learning-Blog/2015/03/Debunk-This-People-Remember-10-Percent-of-What-They-Read.

Claim your free gift

by visiting the link below.
Then join the Fearless & Massively Empowered™ Facebook
group for daily accountability and
support while you continue your journey
toward intentional living.

http://drjatun.ontrapages.com/FAMELounge

Facebook: https://www.facebook.com/dr.jatun/
Twitter: @DrJatun
Instagram: @DrJatun
Website: www.drjatun.com

SHARE YOUR THOUGHTS

With the Author: If this book has impacted you in any way, the author would be delighted to hear about it. Send an email to *author@publishyourgift.com*.

Looking for a Speaker? Book the author to speak at your next event by writing to *booking@publishyourgift.com*.

Discover great books, exclusive offers, and more at
www.PublishYourGift.com

Connect with us on social media

@publishyourgift

www.ingramcontent.com/pod-product-compliance
Lightning Source LLC
Chambersburg PA
CBHW071524080526
44588CB00011B/1548